Published 1979 by Warwick Press, 730 Fifth Avenue,
New York, New York 10019
First published in Great Britain by
Angus and Robertson, 1978
Copyright © 1978 by Grisewood & Dempsey Ltd.
Printed in Italy by New Interlitho, Milan
6 5 4 3 2 1   All rights reserved
Library of Congress Catalog Card No. 78–68538
ISBN 0–531–09154–6 lib. bdg.
ISBN 0–531–09143–0

The Tiger

Story by
JENNIFER JUSTICE

Pictures by
GRAHAM ALLEN

WARWICK PRESS

It was dawn in a grassy clearing in the forest. Monkeys and birds called and chattered high in the nearby trees. The sun rose higher and the air grew hot.

Hidden in the sun-burnt grass, the tigress watched and waited. A deer was grazing not far away. The tigress crept slowly forwards, crouched low on her belly. Her movement hardly stirred the long grass. The deer went on grazing. Little by little, the tigress moved closer.

The deer lifted its head for a moment to sniff the air for danger; but even as it did so, the tigress pounced, her claws spread wide. The helpless animal was knocked to the ground. One quick bite on the neck and it was dead.

Though the deer was nearly as big as she was, the tigress managed to drag it deep into the forest where her meal would not be disturbed. She ate for the first time in four days.

When the tigress had eaten her fill, she rested. She lay in the shade to keep cool. Sunlight found its way through the thick roof of green leaves and dappled the forest floor.

The tigress could hardly be seen as she lay under the trees, panting slightly in the noonday heat. All at once her ears pricked up as she heard a low, coughing roar in the trees close by. Then the bushes parted and another tiger stepped out into a patch of sunlight.

The second tiger was a male. He was bigger than the tigress; long and sleek and powerful.

He approached the tigress slowly and carefully. The tigress pretended not to notice him, and lay with her eyes half closed. The tiger moved closer. He wanted to mate with her, but first he had to be sure that she was ready to mate and would not attack him.

The tigress did want a mate. So, instead of attacking him, she let him stay with her.

The tigress and her mate stayed together for ten days. They hunted at night when it was cool. In the heat of the day they rested by the river. Sometimes they waded into the water. They even swam a little.

One morning, they heard the roar of another tiger. He was looking for a mate. As he came closer, the tigress's mate growled a warning. He bounded across to the rival with teeth and claws bared. The other tiger gave a sharp "whoof" of surprise and fear, then turned away.

    One day the tiger padded off into the forest. The tigress would not see him again. So she set off all alone to find a safe place in which to have her cubs. She traveled a long way through the forest, resting only in the mid-day heat. She did not eat for days at a time.

    At last the tigress reached a rocky hill. The weight of the cubs inside her made her feel tired as she climbed slowly up the rocky slope. Near the top she found a dry cave. It would be a good place to have her cubs.

For the next few days the tigress stayed close to the cave. She hunted and ate well; when her cubs arrived she would not be able to leave them to find food.

One night, three small, helpless cubs were born. They had their mother's black stripes but their eyes were firmly shut. The tigress suckled them and kept them clean and warm. After a few days she began to feel hungry, but she would not leave the cubs, even to hunt.

Soon the cubs opened their eyes and began to explore their cave home. But they were still too young to leave the cave. By now the tigress was hungry and thin. If she did not have some food herself she would not be able to feed the cubs. It was time to go hunting.

Leaving the cubs sheltered behind a rock in the cave, the tigress started down the hill. She was so weak with hunger that she did not notice the wild dogs prowling nearby. The dogs were hungry too. One of them saw the tigress leave and went towards the cave, sniffing the ground.

The dog entered the cool, dark cave. He sniffed the air. There was a strong scent of tiger, but nothing to be seen. The cubs were well hidden. Two of them were asleep, but the third was awake. The little cub nosed his way round the rock and headed for the daylight. As he did so, the dog caught sight of him. In seconds the beast had seized the cub in his jaws and carried it from the cave.

At dawn the tigress returned to the cave. Her hunt had been successful, and she had hidden the remains of her kill. Her nose caught the scent of the dog. She went straight to the two cubs hidden behind the rocks. The third cub was gone.

Without waiting, she took the cubs gently in her mouth. She carried them, one by one, out of the cave and down the hill to a dense grass thicket. There they would be safe if the dog returned.

Day by day, the cubs grew bigger and bolder. They began to explore the hillside, watched over by the tigress. One of their favorite games was to pounce on their mother's long tail as she swished it slowly from side to side. They had many other games. In one, they stalked each other, their small, round bellies nearly touching the ground. Head and neck flattened, one cub would creep slowly towards the other. Then it would leap into the air and land on top of the other cub.

The cubs did not hurt each other. By stalking each other in play, they learned the skills their mother used in hunting. When the time came for them to leave their mother, they would be able to stalk and kill prey for themselves.

One evening the tigress and her cubs set out into the forest. The cubs kept stopping along the way. One pounced on a lizard that scuttled from under a rock. But he had no time to catch another, for the tigress moved steadily on.

Suddenly the tigress sniffed the air. She caught the scent of a large animal moving about in the clearing ahead. It was a buffalo.

The cubs stayed behind the tigress, as she crept forward. The wind was blowing towards her, so the buffalo did not catch her scent. It was a heavy beast with a pair of dangerous horns. She edged forward until she was close enough to strike.

As she sprang, the buffalo twisted its head. One of its horns caught her shoulder. The tigress clawed at its back and tried to get a grip with her teeth, but the buffalo was too strong for her. Stunned, she fell back to the ground. The buffalo lumbered off.

The tigress had had a lucky escape. Limping, she padded slowly back to where the cubs were hiding. That night all they had to eat was a single fish which the tigress scooped from the river with her paw.

The months went by. The cubs now joined their mother on all her hunts. Sometimes she brought down the prey and then stepped back to let the cubs make the kill.

When the cubs were a year old, the bigger of the two went off one night to hunt on his own. He followed a path to the family's favorite spot by the river. There he crouched quietly in the bushes.

He did not have long to wait. A family of wild pigs came down to the river to drink. One of them moved along the bank towards the tiger's hiding place. The young tiger sprang. The squeals of his victim sent the other pigs running, but the cub held his prey fast. He had made his first kill.

The cub dragged the body of the pig to a small ravine. He pushed it under a bush to hide it from the vultures which were always on the lookout for a fresh kill. Then he made off into the forest to fetch his mother and the other cub. They would share the meal with him.

After their meal, the tigers rested. From now on, the cubs would hunt more often on their own. But it would be another year before they left their mother.

When the time came for the cubs to leave, the tigress would be ready to mate again. Soon a new family of tigers would roam the forest.

Tiger Facts

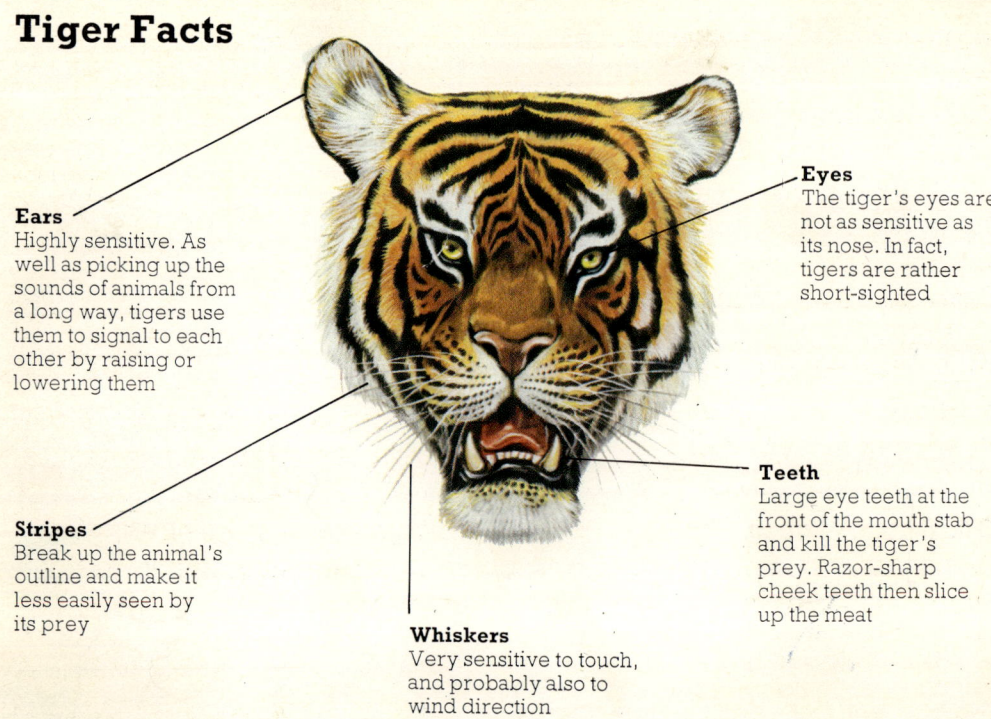

Ears
Highly sensitive. As well as picking up the sounds of animals from a long way, tigers use them to signal to each other by raising or lowering them

Eyes
The tiger's eyes are not as sensitive as its nose. In fact, tigers are rather short-sighted

Stripes
Break up the animal's outline and make it less easily seen by its prey

Teeth
Large eye teeth at the front of the mouth stab and kill the tiger's prey. Razor-sharp cheek teeth then slice up the meat

Whiskers
Very sensitive to touch, and probably also to wind direction

A Magnificent Hunter

The tiger is the largest member of the cat family. Adult males can weigh over 500 pounds. The females are always somewhat smaller.

The tiger's stripes merge with the waving grasses or shrubs. This is especially true in the dim light of dusk, when the tiger does much of its hunting. Deer, pigs, and antelopes are the tiger's main food, but it also kills large buffaloes from time to time and even goes fishing occasionally.

The tiger is a marvelous hunter, using its ears to detect its prey and then padding silently towards it. When it is within a few yards, the tiger bounds forward at high speed. With claws now outstretched, it leaps on its victim and kills it with one blow of a paw or one bite on the neck.

Tiger Types

Tigers live in several different parts of Asia, as you can see from the map. There are several different races or varieties. The

largest ones live in the cold, mountainous areas of Siberia and northern China. These northern tigers are rather pale and they have long fur to keep them warm. Caspian tigers live in reed swamps around the Caspian Sea. Indian tigers live in both forest and grassland, while the Sumatran tigers live in dense forests. The tiger in the story is an Indian tiger.

Old Sabre-Tooth

During the Great Ice Age, there lived a tiger with enormous, dagger-like teeth in its upper jaws. Known a the sabre-tooth tiger, it could open its mouth extremely wide. It probably used its great teeth to stab mammoths and other thick-skinned animals living in those cold times.

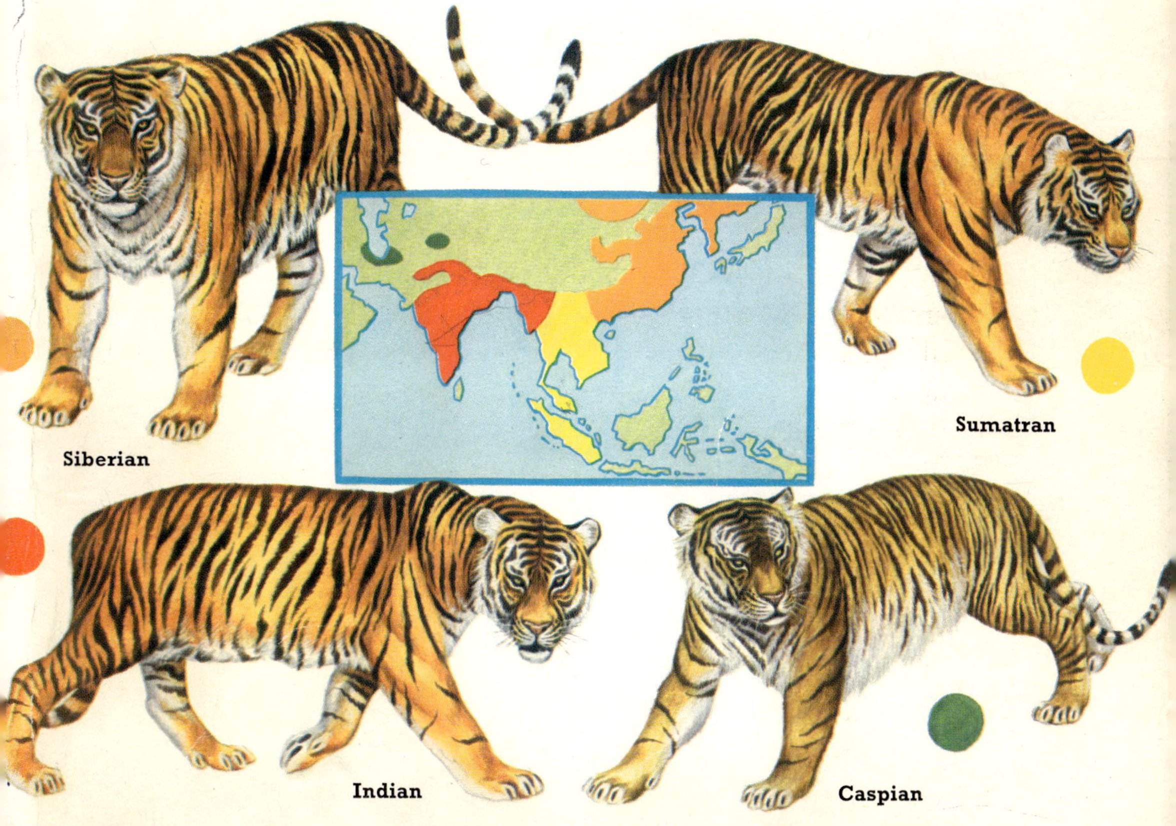

Siberian

Sumatran

Indian

Caspian